D1223223

SUPER SPORTS

Snow Sports

DAVID JEFFERIS

RAINTREE
STECK-VAUGHN
PUBLISHERS

A Harcourt Company

Austin   New York
www.raintreesteckvaughn.com

Published by Raintree Steck-Vaughn Publishers, an imprint of Steck-Vaughn Company

Library of Congress Cataloging-in-Publication Data

Jefferis, David.
    Snow sports / David Jefferis.
        p. cm. -- (Super sports)
    Includes bibliographical references and index.
    ISBN 0-7398-4342-7
        1. Winter sports--Juvenile literature. [1. Winter sports. 2. Skis and skiing.] I. Title. II. Super sports (Austin, Tex.)

GV841.15 .J44 2001
796.9--dc21   2001016099

Acknowledgments
We wish to thank the following individuals and organizations for their help and assistance and for supplying material in their collections:
All Sport, Alpha Archive, Denis Balibouse, Al Bello, Bombardier Recreational Products, Erich Brenter, Buzz Pictures, Shaun Botterill, Simon Bruty, Ulrich Grill, Nick Groves, Mike Hewitt, Jed Jacobsohn, Otto Kasper, Lou Martin, Richard Martin, Darren McNamara, Francois Portmann, Mike Powell, Nick Rawcliffe, Red Bull Communications Centre, Pascal Rondeau, Nikolai Seavey, Jamie Squire, Stock Shot, Vandystadt Agency, Yamaha Motor Co, Zoom Agency

Diagrams by Gavin Page

Printed in China and bound in the United States.

1 2 3 4 5 6 7 05 04 03 02 01

▲ Snowmobiles are used for all kinds of transportation in snowy countries. Snowmobile racing is also popular.

Contents

 Look out for the Super Sports symbol

Look for the skier symbol in boxes like this.
Here you will find extra snow sport facts, stories,
and useful tips for beginners.

World of Snow Sports

There are many different snow sports. They are lots of fun to do and a great way to stay fit.

▲ Snowboards are almost as popular as skis at some resorts.

For most snow sports you will need skis of one shape or another. These help you glide easily across the snow.

Whizzing down mountains is called alpine, or downhill skiing. Nordic, or cross-country, skiing is just like walking, but on skis. It is slower than downhill skiing, but it's hard work. So cross-country skiers need lots of energy.

▼ Cross-country skiing is like walking on skis.

▶ Huskies are bred as working dogs in cold countries. They can also be used for sled races.

▲ Ski poles help skiers balance and turn. Goggles protect the eyes from glare.

▶ At most resorts, skiers reach the ski slopes by riding in chairlifts like the ones shown here, or in cable cars.

Downhill and Slalom Skiing

▲ Racers are timed from the moment they leave the starting gate.

Downhill racing is a very fast ski event over a long course. Slaloms are races in which skiers twist and turn along a winding downhill course.

▼ Great strength is needed to keep control in the turns of a slalom course.

Downhill skiers can reach speeds of 62 miles per hour (100 kmph) or more, while racing down a wide, sweeping course. The course is marked by pairs of poles, called gates. Downhill racers use curved poles that fit around their bodies, and they must wear safety helmets.

In slalom races, skiers race down a bending course, zigzagging between gates as they go. Skiers need to be skilled at making turns as fast and as tight as possible.

▲ Downhill racing slopes are wide and open. This allows a skier to reach high speed without the risk of hitting an obstacle.

 Snow speak

Snow sports have their own special words. Here are some of them:

Binding Safety fitting that joins a ski boot to a ski or snowboard.

Edge Metal strip along each side of a ski. Gives grip in turns.

Fall line Route straight down the steepest part of a ski slope.

Trail Area set out for skiers, with smoothed and cleared snow.

Schuss Skiing downhill fast, with skis parallel to each other.

Traverse Skiing across the fall line, rather than straight down.

Cross-Country Skiing

Cross-country ski courses include sections that are flat, as well as uphill and downhill. Skiers use special skis that are longer than Alpine skis.

▲ Biathlon races combine a tough cross-country course with rifle sharp-shooting.

▶ Cross-country racing is very hard work on flat and uphill sections.

To glide smoothly along, cross-country skiers either slide on their skis and push forward with their poles, or use a skating movement. Races cover various distances, from short sprint events to long marathons.

Cross-country ski routes are often prepared using machines that crush flattened paths through the snow.

Uphill climb by herringbone

A cross-country ski has a special surface. This helps it grip when a skier goes up gentle slopes.

On gentle hills, skiers use a "herringbone" movement. The skis are angled into a v-shape, so the edges push into the snow for extra grip.

Skiers have to sidestep up steep hills, which is much slower.

v-shaped marks left by skis going uphill

▲ A cross-country racer keeps going even though a big snowstorm is coming.

Freestyle Stunts

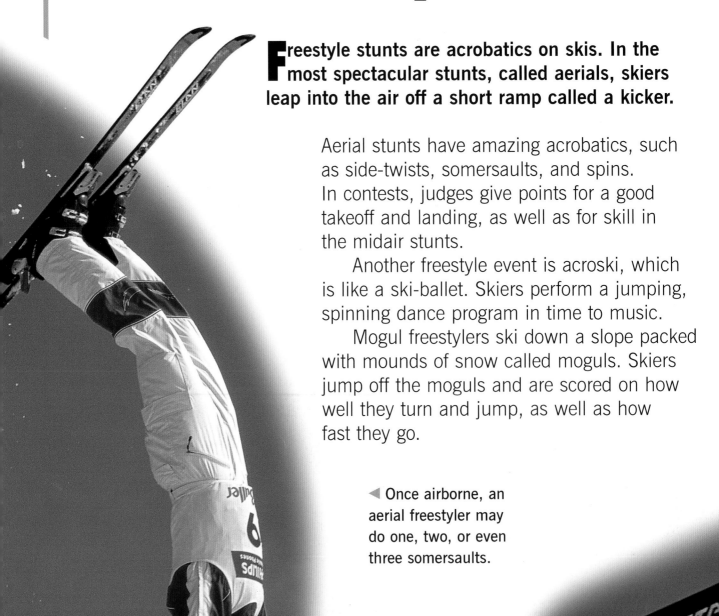

Freestyle stunts are acrobatics on skis. In the most spectacular stunts, called aerials, skiers leap into the air off a short ramp called a kicker.

Aerial stunts have amazing acrobatics, such as side-twists, somersaults, and spins. In contests, judges give points for a good takeoff and landing, as well as for skill in the midair stunts.

Another freestyle event is acroski, which is like a ski-ballet. Skiers perform a jumping, spinning dance program in time to music.

Mogul freestylers ski down a slope packed with mounds of snow called moguls. Skiers jump off the moguls and are scored on how well they turn and jump, as well as how fast they go.

◄ Once airborne, an aerial freestyler may do one, two, or even three somersaults.

Smoothing the trail

At big resorts, the trails are prepared every night to be ready for the next day.

One of the most important tools is a trail-maker, like the machine shown here. The driver scoops snow neatly into place with a big snowplow.

Trail-makers cannot tackle the steepest slopes. Here snow may form mounds, or moguls—perfect for mogul freestylers.

Wide tracks give the trail-maker grip on most slopes.

▼ A freestyler spins around and around in a movement called the helicopter.

Ski Jump

▲ Ski-jump ramps at dawn, ready for an early start to the day's events.

Ski jumping is a sport for the brave. Jumpers ski down a steep ramp called the in-run. Then, they shoot into the air for a distance of 230 feet (70 m) or more, before they land.

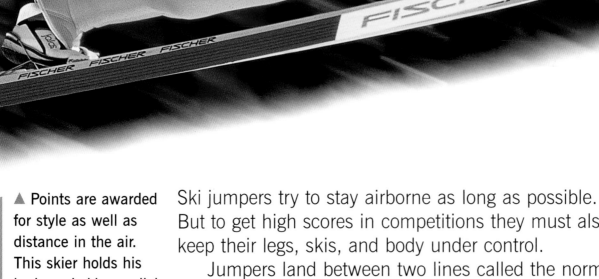

▲ Points are awarded for style as well as distance in the air. This skier holds his body and skis parallel to one another. But holding the front tips apart in a V-shape is popular, too.

Ski jumpers try to stay airborne as long as possible. But to get high scores in competitions they must also keep their legs, skis, and body under control.

Jumpers land between two lines called the norm and table points. It's dangerous to go much farther, since there may not be room to stop safely.

Jump skis are based on cross-country skis, but are longer, wider, and heavier. Grooves under the skis help to give the skier control in flight.

▲ Jumpers go down the in-run crouched low to build up speed.

Top marks for a stylish jump

Ski jumpers lose points for faults on takeoff, flight, and landing. If a jumper touches the snow with a hand when landing, for example, that counts as a fault. Most ski-jumps are between 230 feet (70 m) and 394 feet (120 m). Ski-flying is another event, that is scored only on the distance flown.

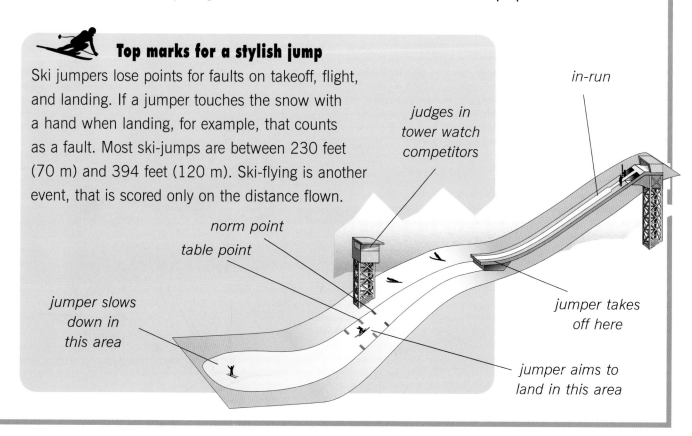

in-run

judges in tower watch competitors

norm point

table point

jumper slows down in this area

jumper takes off here

jumper aims to land in this area

Snowboards

Snowboarders use a wide, surfboard-shaped ski instead of a pair of long, narrow skis. Snowboards are great for doing all sorts of aerial stunts.

▲ Beginners start on gentle nursery slopes.

Boarders stand sideways with their boots locked on to the board. They use their body and arms to help keep their balance.

Steering a board is like using the rudder on a boat. The board is turned to the left or right when the boarder pushes with the toes or heel of his back foot.

There are downhill and freestyle events for snowboards. Many resorts have trails set aside for these.

◄ This snowboarder is a "regular"—he rides with his left foot forward. Some boarders lead with the right foot and are known as "goofies."

Riders of all shapes and sizes can find a board to fit.

14

▼ Snowboards are high-fashion gear and come in a great variety of different colors and patterns.

▲ Many snowboarders learn skills such as "hanging air," shown here. It's like a snow version of skateboarding.

Building a snowboard

Boards and skis look simple enough, but designing them is a skilled job. They are made of layers of material, joined together to make a strong type of sandwich.

The center, or core, is usually made of many thin layers of wood—often ash or birch. Other materials surround the core to finish off the board's construction.

A good board is strong but has spring in it to make jumps and turns easier.

Bobsled and Luge

These are toboggans built for racing. They hurtle down a smooth, icy course at speeds of over 62 mph (100 kmph).

Bobsleds race, one at a time, down an icy run, at speeds of 62 mph (100 kmph). The crew pushes the bobsled down the run to build up speed before leaping in. They wear spiked shoes to grip the ice.

Speeding down the run, the front rider steers and the person at the back works the brakes. In a four-person sled, the two middle crew members help to steady the sled as it goes around corners.

A luge is like a toboggan. Riders lie on their backs during a race. There are also two-place luges. That's the luge where one rider lies on top of the other!

◄ A two-person team crouches behind the bodywork of a bobsled. The driver steers. The rear person puts on the brakes when they are needed.

Losing control at over 62 mph (100 kmph).

A luge is little more than a plastic and metal seat. It is built to slide down a smooth, icy track called a run.

Riders lie back on the luge and go down the run feet-first. They hang on to a strap and steer by leaning from side to side. Crashes happen regularly, but luckily serious injuries are rare.

A helmet is very important in case of a crash.

▲ A team runs hard to launch a bobsled. The front two crew members push the sled with handles that fold neatly away during the race.

Snowmobiles

Snowmobiles speed across the snow like motorbikes. The front skis are used for steering, and an engine provides the power.

▲ Riders lean into corners to stay upright. Wide front skis help keep the snowmobile level.

The first snowmobiles were made in 1959. They were a speedy way to travel in snowy countries.

Modern snowmobiles can shoot across the snow at speeds of 62 mph (100 kmph) or more. They have skis at the front for steering and a track whizzing around under the seat that pushes them forward.

Today, snowmobile racing is a popular snow sport with dozens of contests taking place throughout the winter months.

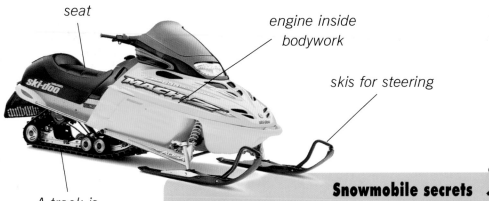

seat

engine inside bodywork

skis for steering

A track is used instead of wheels.

Snowmobile secrets

The snowmobile's success lies in its skis and wide rubber drive track. The track grips the snow much better than wheels and sends the snowmobile shooting forward. The skis let the driver steer the machine almost anywhere, without it sinking into the snow. The skis are turned with the handlebars.

Snowmobiles are used for all sorts of jobs. For example, polar explorers use them for towing supplies.

► Racing snowmobiles need thorough checking. The rear track can be fitted with metal spikes for extra grip.

spiked rubber track

▼ Only an expert rider can perform high-speed stunts like this safely.

A plastic screen keeps cold wind off the rider's chest.

Snow Explorers

Making trips into distant mountain areas is a great idea for people who want more than a few days skiing in a resort area.

Careful planning is essential for people who ski in high mountains. If a storm blows up suddenly, it may be some time before help arrives.

It's possible to be snowed in for several days, so emergency food supplies are necessary. A tough, stormproof tent that's quick to put up is important, too.

▲ Snowshoes let walkers travel in soft snow. They used to be made of wood and strips of leather. New designs are in metal and plastic.

◀ Backpacks are loaded carefully for good balance on the move.

Here's an exciting adventure for ski explorers. They fly into a distant mountain area by plane or helicopter.

The days are spent skiing, using maps to stay on course. The nights are spent in lightweight tents that keep out the cold. After a week in the snow, the explorers are picked up and flown home.

A lightweight tent folds flat and packs into a small bag.

► The air may be cold, but skiing cross-country can be hot work. This is especially true for uphill parts. There may be snowstorms, so using good survival gear is very important.

Dogsled Races

husky

wolf

▲ The ancestor of the husky is the wolf. Both animals can survive easily in the cold.

In Alaska, huskies were once used as work dogs to carry freight and mail. Today, huskies also go racing!

The most famous husky race is the Iditerod, which is held in Alaska every March. This long race is nearly 1,056 miles (1700 km). Teams of 12-18 dogs usually complete the race in about ten days. Each dog team has a musher, a person in charge.

The rules are strict, especially when it comes to the dogs' health. Each dog is checked for good health before and during the race.

▶ Teams of huskies are harnessed together with a lead dog at the front.

 What's in a name?

The Iditerod gets its name from a word used by Native Americans of the Athabasca tribe. It means "the distant place" and was first used to describe inland hunting grounds.

The dog-team drivers are known as mushers, a term that comes from the French word for "walk," or "marcher." In the nineteenth and early twentieth centuries, Alaskans described almost any travel over snow as mushing.

▲ A team of huskies
is expensive to feed.
These dogs earn their
keep between races
by hauling tourists
on sightseeing rides.

*Harnesses join
the huskies to
the sled.*

23

New Ideas

▲ The snowbone is a board for beginners. Riders hold the handle and can jump off if they make a mistake.

New snow equipment is invented all the time. Lightweight skis make skiing easier and safer, and modern fabrics help to make lighter, warmer clothing.

New equipment makes learning to ski easier for beginners. For example, short skis are lighter than normal ones and easier to use. Once you have learned the basics, it isn't difficult to learn to use full-size skis.

Ski safety is very important. Wearing a helmet is becoming popular, especially for children.

As ski equipment improves, skiers are able to set new records for speed.

▼ Heli-skiing allows skiers to reach distant peaks, but it is an expensive sport.

◄ Speed skiing is the fastest ski sport. Here a speed skier wears a plastic suit made to slip through the air easily. He is trying it out in a lab where designers test how well the suit works.

specially shaped helmet, designed to slice through the air

► Using speed equipment like this, it is possible to go faster than 137 mph (220 kmph).

Snow Sport Facts

▲ A skibob rider at speed.

Here are some facts and stories from the world of snow sports.

The first skiers

Skiing started to be popular only about 120 years ago. But skis have been used in some places for much longer.

The oldest ski in the world was found in Sweden.

It is thought to be about 4,500 years old. It is made of pine and has a slot for a foot to fit in, with holes for bindings. There are also rock carvings showing ski-hunters that may be even older.

Hillside ski jumps

Ski sports began in Norway, when Sondre Norheim started ski jumping in the 1840s. He was the first skier to jump down steep hillsides.

Norheim also improved ski equipment, which helped him win prizes in an 1868 ski competition.

Speedy luge...

The top speed for a luge run is held by a Norwegian, Asle Strand. In 1982, he hurtled downhill at over 85 mph (137 kmph).

...but faster skibob

Skibobs are like bicycles on skis. Riders use mini-skis clipped to their boots to help them balance when they corner. But skibobs can go much faster than a bike with wheels. In 1999, a Swiss skibob rider reached 107 mph (173 kmph).

◄ Biathlon races mix a cross-country course with rifle sharp-shooting.

◀ A luge racer starts a run with a mighty heave at the start gate.

Hero of the snow

The Iditerod dogsled race in Alaska takes place every year in memory of a husky called Balto.

In 1925, Balto led a dog-team taking medicine to Nome, where there was an outbreak of a disease known as diphtheria. The weather was terrible, with blinding snowstorms, very high winds, and icy-cold temperatures.

The 674 mile (1085 km) route was covered by a number of husky relay teams. Balto led the final team into Nome, after a 53 mile (85 km) run through the snow.

Finland's mega-race

The world's biggest ski race is held in Finland each year, and thousands take part. The cross-country course is 46 m (75 km long). One year 13,226 people entered! Most people finished the race.

Cresta run

The Cresta run in Switzerland, is the home of bobsled racing. The fastest sled has covered the 3,976 foot (1212 m) course in 50.09 seconds.

One-day endurance

Finland comes up tops for many snow events, including skiing non-stop for 24 hours. In 1988, Seppo-Juhani Savolainen covered 258 miles (415.5 km) in this timed event—an average speed of more than 10.6 mph (17 kmph).

▶ In 1922, 15-year-old Canadian Joseph-Armand Bombardier built an early type of snowmobile. His "snow-sleigh" (right) was powered by a propeller.
Later, in 1959, Bombardier's company launched the modern-style snowmobile, which was called a Ski-Doo.

front runners turn to steer   *engine*   *propeller at back*

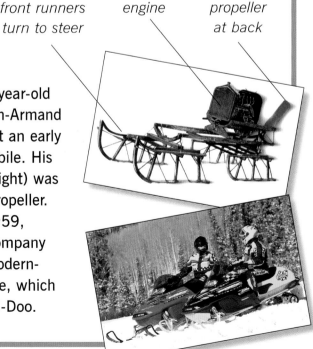

▲ Freestyle aerial.

Snow Sport Words

Here are some special terms used in this book.

alpine skiing (AL-pine SKEE-ing)
Alpine, or downhill, is the name for skiing down mountains. The other type of skiing is cross-country, or nordic.

biathlon (bye-ATH-lon)
A biathlon may combine cross-country with rifle sharp-shooting.

bindings (BINDE-ingz)
Clips that join boots to skis or snowboards. Bindings release if a skier falls to avoid breaking a leg or ankle.

chairlift
A system of chairs that carry skiers up mountains. The chairs hang from a cable that moves between metal towers.

▶ Bindings join boots to skis.

edge (ej)
The metal sides of a ski. They are tougher than the rest of the ski, and take the strain of cornering by carving into the snow or ice.

fall line (FAWL line)
A route leading straight down the steepest part of a slope. Crossing the fall line from side to side is called traversing.

freestyle (free-stile)
Acrobatics on skis or on a snowboard. There are three types of freestyle events: aerials, acroski, and mogul.

gate (gate)
A pair of marker poles used in ski racing. There is also a starting gate.

heli-skiing (HEL-uh-SKEE-ing)
Using a helicopter to give skiers a lift up to a distant or very high slope.

herringbone (HER-ing bohn)
A method of climbing up a gentle slope on skis. Skis are put into a v-shape so the skier can press back into the snow to get up the hill.

mogul (MOH-gull)
A mound of snow created by skiers turning on a steep slope. Lots of them in one area is called a mogul field.

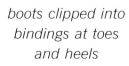

boots clipped into bindings at toes and heels

musher (MUHSH-ur)
The driver in charge of a dogsled team. The term comes from the French word *marcher,* "to walk."

nordic skiing
(NOR-dik SKEE-ing)
See alpine skiing.

norm point (nohrm point)
The first of three landing points on a ski-jump slope. A jumper tries to land at the table point. The critical point is the last point where there is room to stop safely.

parallel ski (PA-ruh-lel skee)
Skiing with skis that are the same distance apart.

poles (pohlz)
Sticks used by skiers to help with balance, especially when they are turning sharply.

run (ruhn)
A ski or snowboard course, or the icy slope of a bobsled or luge course.

schuss (shoohs)
A straight-line course often straight down a fall line.

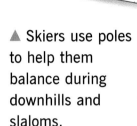

▲ Skiers use poles to help them balance during downhills and slaloms.

slalom (SLAH-lum)
A downhill race which weaves through marker gates. Also describes a zigzag downhill course.

snowshoe (SNOH-shoo)
An extra-large outer frame, made to spread the weight of a person on the snow. It is often attached to and worn under a snowboot.

trail (trayl)
A ski trail that is specially prepared for skiers.

◄ Cable cars do a job similar to chairlifts. Skiers ride up the mountain in small cabins.

Snow Science

There is a lot to learn about snow and the science behind snow sports.

◄ A ski slides easily because it has a slippery bottom. These are usually made of plastic, but they may need waxing to keep them smooth.

The front ends of skis are called tips.

▲ Snowboards also need to be smooth.

Why do skis need to be smooth?

Smooth skis slide much more easily on snow, which allows a skier to go faster. This experiment shows you the difference between a rough surface and a smooth surface.

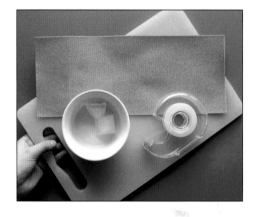

1 You need two ice cubes, a sheet of sandpaper, a kitchen cutting board, and some tape.

2 Lay the sandpaper on one side of the board. Tape it down at each end to keep it in place.

◀ Powder snow forms when the temperature is well below freezing.

Where does snow come from?

Snow falls as flakes, each one made up of ice crystals. The ice crystals come in different shapes, such as needles and hexagons. They are formed from the water vapor inside clouds. All snowflakes have a six-sided shape, but each flake's pattern is slightly different.

▲ Snowflakes come in many shapes, but all have six sides. There are many different kinds of snow—from fine, dry powder to heavy, wet slush.

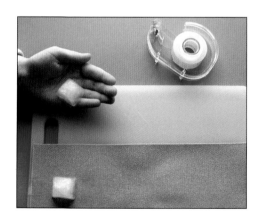

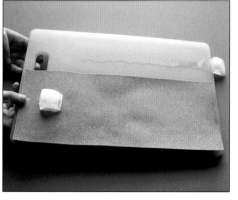

3 Carefully lay the two ice cubes at one end, one on the board, the other on the sandpaper.

4 Gently lift the board to make a slope. See which cube whizzes to the bottom of the slope first.

31

Index

J
796.9
Jef   Jefferis, David

        Snow sports